THE POWER
of the
FIGHTER

THE POWER
of the
FIGHTER

Shelton Forman
VISOLOGY PUBLISHING

Copyright © 2020 Shelton Foreman
All rights reserved. No part of this book may be reproduced or transmitted in any form or by any means, electronic or mechanical, including photocopy, recording, or by any information storage and retrieval system with the exception of a reviewer who may quote brief passages in a review to be printed in a blog, newspaper or magazine without written permission from the author. Address inquiries to: support@thepowerofthefigher.com
Published with assistance from Expected End Entertainment
ISBN: 978-0-578-75007-1

Printed in the United States of America

CONTENTS

	PREFACE	1
1	BE AWARE OF YOUR SURROUNDINGS	3
2	DO NOT RUN	7
3	FOCUS ON THE VISION	13
4	KEEP THE DESIRE	19
5	ENVISION SUCCESS	23
6	AFFIRM YOURSELF	29
7	BE CONSTRUCTIVE	33
8	ACCEPTING THE WIN	39
	ABOUT THE AUTHOR	44

To my mother, brother, and my family, you all mean the world to me!!!

ACKNOWLEDGMENTS

When I began to write this book, the year was 2009 and unhappiness was a part of my daily mood. Every relationship and path desired were nothing less than challenging. Life was tough and I refused to fold at any cost. Life has a way of humbling you through its lessons, both good and bad.

I would be remiss if I did not honor God. I am thankful for his strength, love, and the power. I would like to acknowledge my loving mother, Phyllis Lawrence, and my resilient and patient brother Xavier Lawrence. I would like to thank my family; you are the best support system a man could ever have. I am truly surrounded by love and you all have taught me how to fight for my goals, aspirations, and my life through resilience. To my lovely and beautiful grandmother Beatrice Lawrence, thank you for your wisdom and teaching me how to face things head-on without fear. Lastly, I thank the readers for purchasing this book. I hope you discover the fighter in you to conquer any and every challenge you may face.

Be blessed and enjoy!

Shelton Foreman

SHELTON FOREMAN

PREFACE

SHELTON FOREMAN

When you think of fighters, you may think about a league of extraordinary men or women who are physically ready for any altercation or unforeseen and unfavorable situations. Fighters are ready for any and everything and they're fully aware of unfavorable situations. Life has a way of fighting individuals without providing mercy or warning. Most fights begin within and these internal fights simply cannot be ignored. Some people have consistent battles that no one knows about. The Power of the Fighter is unmatched, regardless of the challenges presented. It is an unparalleled power than can be tested, but never tamed.

CHAPTER ONE

BE AWARE OF YOUR SURROUNDINGS

You often hear, "Things were going well until a bad situation hit me by surprise." Life is unpredictable with its twists, turns and sometimes unfair situations. Some situations present themselves at the most inopportune times. We all get comfortable in life with little or no thought to the possibility that things could change in a split moment.

If you think about some of the greatest physical fighters such as Joe Frazier, George Foreman, or even Floyd Mayweather, they were often heavily prepared to win but they also studied scenarios, opponents, and techniques. Preparation is awareness and being knowledgeable of a possible outcome. We can never escape the threat of life beating us until we are lifeless. However, we can be proactive instead of reactive in any situation.

I met a businessman who held a Ph.D., but due to a series of unfortunate events, he was also homeless. One would think education, business acumen, and personal pizzazz would lead him to a wealthy and great life until death. This gentleman told me his story about having it all and losing it all, then giving up due to the pressures of life. He was simply unaware of his internal power and did not enjoy having to endure the pressures of life.

We all enjoy the waves of life when we are simply riding the waves of fruitfulness and fulfilment. What about when your money is gone, and hope appears to be at a great distance or seemingly far-fetched? It may sound cliché, but true fighters are ready to face life's temporary and external situations with resilience.

Some people may ask, "Why me?" I, too, have asked this question. However, over the years, I have realized that my "Try Me" approach has helped me conquer some unfavorable situations and events. It is not easy to develop mental fortitude during a storm. David was faced with a monumental task when he was promoted to supervisor at 16. He had to lead a passionate group of his peers and individuals that undermined his authority. He was intimated by his new role until his boss told him, "Rise to the occasion or be demoted." David implemented new rules and changed his leadership style.

You can't control fate, but your attitude could adjust accordingly. Every problem has a solution and if you face problems, issues, and trouble head on you, will develop the "try me" attitude.

Bearing pain and unfortunate events are all a part of the process of life and one can't escape those lessons. Problems have a way of interfering with your current and future perspectives. However, a positive perspective can open doors for a positive and fulfilling life.

> *"Let us not look back in anger, nor forward in fear, but around in awareness."*
>
> **James Thurber**

History has proven that many people have overcome many indifferent situations regardless of the opposition or the oppression. President Lincoln had a host of failures before becoming president. He experienced deaths in his family, immense pain, and a nervous breakdown before his presidency.

What gives one the power to go on when we are physically, mentally, and physically tired? Emotional intelligence begins within an individual and ignites the fighter in you to become a true overcomer. You may be facing uncomfortable events and situations that are indeed frequent and erratic. They might even seem unbearable. However, awareness and optimism will diminish doubt. Some may say it's easier said than done and in many cases that might be true. But triumph is a story of trials and overcoming them. Here is a list of subjects that will remind you of major areas that can help you seek self-awareness in your everyday life for improvement.

Major Subjects:
- Understand your life story so far
- Accept your past: the good, bad, and the ugly.
- Create a daily meditation or prayer session
- Seek honest feedback
- Find more than one thing that makes you happy
- Seek your passion wholeheartedly
- Love without limits
- Live unapologetically

CHAPTER TWO

DO NOT RUN

There was a kind woman who was dealing with a divorce and Stage III cancer at the same time. Like many others, she felt like life had unfairly dealt her a bad hand. She was a grateful woman who was always good to others. She cried daily, lost her hair, hope, and her will to live through her situation. But somewhere in the back of her mind, she knew that she could beat the diagnosis and it was not a death wish.

Alone, she considered herself to be a strong-willed person. However, she asked friends and family to help her to face the painful and mentally draining process of defeating her challenges. She began to go out regularly, exploring unforeseen places, and living life out loud. She manifested her thoughts of living and fulfillment and beat cancer six months after diagnosis. She could have easily run from life and its unjust effects and given up her will to live. But the fighter in her choose life and abundance.

Some people cringe at the thought of things not going their way. However, running will guarantee the problem will return. Facing issues and being upfront about either outcome is often the story of the overcomer.

Life is a gamble. You can get hurt, but people die in plane crashes, lose their arms and legs in car accidents, and suffer other tragedies every day. It's the same with fighters: some die, some get hurt, some go on. You just don't let yourself believe it will happen to you.

Muhammad Ali Muhammed Ali, one of the world's greatest fighters ever, was a rhetorical rhymer. But he was also full of strength and power. He was a fighter, but he understood the concept of living. We all have death, pain, and sickness around us. Running from pain or indifferent situations never produced glorious outcomes. Many people praise running and giving up on life and situations because it may feel better than facing the problem directly.

> *"Anxiety weighs down the heart, but a kind word cheers it up." (Proverbs 12:25)*

Have you ever heard of a person who "takes a licking but keeps on ticking?" There was a young man who wanted to be successful but who hated his job and his current situation. He came home every day feeling lackadaisical and unfulfilled with the monotony of his everyday routine. He was strong minded and strong willed and was often judged by his superiors for being a rebel. He was incredibly smart and challenged the status quo with knowledge to improve himself. However, most saw him as a troublemaker when he voiced his opinions and chose an unpopular opinion. He changed jobs for better positions but, as the years went by, he quickly realized he was only running from himself. He decided to seek a collegiate education not for a job but to enhance his business skills. He worked on his intrapersonal and interpersonal skills. Unlike many, he knew how to identify the personal fight within himself.

People often think that searching outside of themselves, changing jobs, removing people, or buying new clothes can change the internal factors of happiness. Why do we run from ourselves when we never can? Why do we blame others about our life when we may indeed be the problem? Some may live their lives to blame others because it's an easier route than looking within. The easy route will lead to stagnate growth within an individual.

Gym enthusiasts may tell you that initially, they found it hard to commit. They may have had plans to lose a certain amount of weight to experience specific gains. They found it hard to focus or to stay on track, so to speak. However, they set realistic goals and made conscious decisions to change their lives and their health. They worked at it and instead of running, they found a new passion that improved their lives.

What external factors would it take to make you change your life today? Think about it and expound about that thought.

Mary was a perfect example of an overweight, mentally ill, and an overall unhappy woman. She did not like her life, her outer appearance, and ignored and validated her mental health diagnoses. Each day, she ate enough for two or three people to suppress the pain of being alone and being abused as a child. She cried and ate to feel comfortable and mask the internal pain. Mary was running from the pain of her childhood, her past, and the way people treated her. How many people are like Mary? They hold on to their past and present pain and mask it with food, drugs, or other crutches. Many may smile every day but are dying slowly on the inside.

THE POWER OF THE FIGHTER

One day, Mary went for a routine checkup and received some potentially devastating health news that changed her perspective about life. She followed up with her specialist about her diagnosis and preventable methods that could turn things around for the better. Mary was instructed to lose 100 pounds or face the possibility of dying in less than two years, just as some of her family members had. She quickly began searching for diet and exercise plans to lose weight. She knew that she did not want an early death, however, she knew her eating habits would be hard to change.

Mary hired a nutritionist to help with the dieting, and a counselor to help her with her mental issues. She decided not to run any longer; masking the problem was too easy and comfortable. She identified the issues and decided to change for her future and for current life experience to create a better life. Mary lost over 150 pounds in one year due to one disdained warning. She committed herself to making the impossible possible without constraints or cognitive reasoning.

> *"The possible is more of a matter of altitude, choosing among the impossible to the possible."*
>
> *S. Foreman*

What if Mary continued to tell herself a story to validate about her condition? Conditioning her brain to think that her way was not determinantal. We often tell ourselves stories to make excuses, thinking it's helping us cope. We may tell ourselves stories about not being good enough, comparing ourselves to our peers or even our parents. Just as successful surfers, one must learn how to surf the uncomfortable waves to become a professional life surfer and/or balancer. The best surfer did not learn how to glide or surf the calm waves; they learned how to conquer the violent waves.

Greatness requires one to commit during volatile or uncertain moments. You may have heard someone say, "Well, did you die?" Okay, death is not funny, but think about it. Did you die after a horrible day? If you are reading this, you are alive, and you were stronger than the situation or situations you faced. Never quit! I know it may sound cliché, but you must commit to not run from the situation, run to it.

Powerful things can happen in the eye of the storm. One could find out what he or she is made of. The amount of optimism is strictly based upon each person's thoughts and willingness to show gratitude for the experience itself. Some of us have seen the commercials where the children in the cancer centers are fighting for their lives. Despite the possibilities of dying, they still have smiles on their faces that could light up any room. Adults can learn so much from these kids, their gratitude, and the ability to face pain as a life lesson.

CHAPTER THREE

FOCUS ON THE VISION

Visionaries are often accused of being unrealistic and out of touch with their life. Some say visionaries live in a fairytale because they believe that everything is always going to be all right. Envisioning your life to be a perfect mirage is not focusing but being pretentious is ideal for achievement.

> *"The greatest danger for most of us is not that our aim too high and we miss it, but that it is too low and we reach it."*
>
> *Michelangelo*

Most children have a great amount of enthusiasm, hope, and faith in themselves. You often see them planning to make that winning game shot or to ride their bike down a death-defying hill without an ounce of fear. They have a certain amount magic within them that is often lost as an adolescent or an adult. This magic is simply a powerful energy that supersedes the idea of failure.

What would you accomplish today if one told you that you could not fail? The fear of failing may hold a lot of us back from accomplishing our goals. We all have something that we would like to accomplish for ourselves or our families. I personally would like to serve in a multifaceted capacity role, whereas I could position all my family and friends so they will never want for anything. I would like to teach them how to think out loud and grow businesses that would become bigger than themselves or their wildest thoughts.

Teachers often ask their pupils, "What would you like to be when you grow up?" Without hesitation, some students proclaim professions that are beyond their neighborhoods, economic status, or current familial situations. Children have an imagination and a hopeful attitude that things will go as planned. However, adults are taught to be realistic, to stick to the plan, and accept societal purposes. We are taught to go to college, get a job, get married and love the so-called dream life. Unfortunately, dreams sometimes are deferred and life throws curveballs. Some people simply fall apart when life throws them lemons because they just don't know what to do with unexpected circumstances.

There was once a successful businessman who had it all…a dream job with a six-figure salary, wife and kids, and a blissful life. One day, he felt a strange feeling in his chest. He ignored it for a few hours, but it became more painful by the minute. Like most men, this gentleman initially refused to go to the hospital. In fact, he went on with his day as usual. While walking to his car to prepare to close a deal, he began to sweat profusely and fainted. He didn't realize he was having a heart attack that would lead to additional complications.

His heart attack, at 32 years old, was an unforeseen situation and was completely shocking to him. Spending time in the hospital for months caused him to lose his dream job, family, and millions of dollars. Amid his illness, his wife left him, and he was left to recovery alone. There were days where the loneliness and despair caused the man to want to die. However, he was a businessman who knew that just as in business, he would have good and bad days and would eventually recover. He began journaling his thoughts and envisioning himself becoming well, which increased his mental fortitude.

Life changed drastically and instead of lying in despair and hopelessness, he decided he would pick up the pieces that were leftover and have gratitude just for living. Not only did he have a hefty savings, he had a strong network of people to assist in his new business consulting firm that could grow while he was recovering. He doubled his income, saved his home, developed a better relationship with his children and lived life like the curveball was never thrown.

Visionaries often understand that life is sometimes sour and unbearable but just like those months in the "red" there are also periods in the "black". However, accepting failure as a learning tool can induce more success. You may question your abilities to succeed or you may ask yourself, do I measure up? If one will succeed, he or she must envision their success as if their goals and dreams have already happened and train their minds to see the best out of any situation.

> *"For as he thinketh in his heart, so is he."*
>
> **Proverbs 23:7**

THE POWER OF THE FIGHTER

What do you think about yourself at this moment? Are you fighting for your goals or living the dream that belongs to someone else? I encourage you to ignite that childhood dream and fight for another chance to succeed. Time is not a lifetime friend and sometimes she presents herself as an enemy. However, nothing can hold you back but you. Dreams and visions are interchangeable. Now is the time to fight for the life that you would like to live. Here is a list of subjects that will remind you of major areas that can help you envision your future.

- ❏ Stay focused on your goals
- ❏ Form your short-term and long-term goals
- ❏ Make an initiative plan to succeed
- ❏ Take the first step without regrets

SHELTON FOREMAN

CHAPTER FOUR

KEEPING THE DESIRE

Some people may find themselves switching from job to job or entering relationships prematurely and ending them abruptly for happiness. Impulsive attitudes and behaviors may be a cover up for a sense of fulfillment. No one can tell you about you and what you need for self-fulfillment. We all hear about the individuals who always start something new, but never finish what they start.

What is your ultimate goal or lifelong desire? Have you written your desires down or have you revisited them lately? Studies have shown that those who write down desires are more likely to pursue them wholeheartedly. The willingness to succeed should burn like an eternal fire. Giving up on life or on a goal just because you may face opposition will diminish your chances to complete anything in life.

> *"The will to win, the desire to succeed, the urge to reach your full potential...these are the keys that will unlock the door to personal excellence."*
>
> **Confucius**

You may run into people who do not have a clue about where they are going or where they have been. Living life day by day without a pretentious meaning must be boring and unfulfilled. Having a will to win may unlock doors and create endless possibilities. So, what do you do when you achieve progress toward your goals then circumstances force you to take five steps back? You must be optimistic and resilient. It does not matter how hard reality seems; you must hold on to your dreams. No matter how old you are, where you're from or what you do for a living, we all share many things in common, including a burning desire to be successful.

Everyone's definition of success may be different. Some people define their success with power, fame, and wealth while others define success as being a faithful and loving person. We all want a level of success to live comfortably. You may have a desire to drive a nice car or to live in a huge house. Sometimes success may be slow in materializing. Other times, it may not come at all. Some may choose to give up or change their whole approach to what success means to them.

A mediocre high school student was faced with a familiar situation that clouded his judgment. He grew up with mediocre grades and was always told that he was not college material. As a kid, the mediocre student always wanted to be successful. He wrote a goal sheet at the age of 13 that was progressive and obtainable. He had plans to attend college and to become a businessman to assist others who were less fortunate, just like him. The years went by and his high school career was filled with various amounts of challenges. However, he graduated, and that chapter was over in a blink of an eye. He applied for several colleges his last semester of high school, getting accepted into several universities with massive scholarships. He knew that his only antidote to poverty was opportunity that he would have to pursue. He enrolled in a four-year program and completed his bachelor's degree and thereafter his master's degree. His burning desire to keep going led him to achieve things many thought he never could. The negative words and actions never dimmed his fire and only encouraged him to achieve more.

Steps for achievement are inclusive of setting deadlines. You may hear a person say, "I would like to take a trip to Paris" but will probably never get their chance. However, the person who says, "I am going to Paris before July 2, 2021", will more than likely get there. A simple date is like creating an action plan.

Here is a list of subjects that will remind you of major areas to ignite your passion and how to keep the desires.

- ❏ Never underestimate your value or power
- ❏ Make a commitment to yourself
- ❏ Keep an open mind
- ❏ Be persistent in all your efforts
- ❏ Be accountable to yourself
- ❏ Always be thankful

CHAPTER FIVE

ENVISION SUCCESS

Skiers and many other athletes often visualize themselves winning without hesitation. Skiers, in particular, will go over every slope, twist, and turn to understand how their bodies would respond. By contrast, life is no different. We all visualize the outcome or scenarios that we want in life. The power of your mind and thoughts are spellbinding.

> *"Whatever you can do or dream you can, begin it. Boldness has genius, and magic and power in it. Begin it."*
>
> **Goethe**

We often hear people tell us to focus so hard that there is no other option but to achieve our goals. However, one can focus so much that they miss the process of goal attainment. The process may seem rigid but, to be successful in creating your dreams, you must believe you're capable. You may call it self-assurance, self-confidence, and self-esteem but one must have the throttle within. It is a deep belief and very much an internal belief that you have the abilities, inner resources, skills, and talents to create your desired outcome. An unwavering faith in yourself in the good and bad times will create good inertia and experiences in your life. Everyone will experience degrees of success, struggle, strife, and pain as each is a part of the living experience.

This is straightforward: Imagine how much easier life

would be if you constantly expected to win in life with more hope than doubt. Experts on the science of success know the brain is a goal-seeking and pretentiously uncompromised muscle. Whatever goal or desire you have in your subconscious mind, and you're willing to work night and day for it, you're bound to achieve it.

Sometimes we just need to make an initial goal of simply thinking about success. Achievement comes with a few steps of action that can lead to leaps and bounds. Are you unhappy about something that is happening in your life right now? Change your perspective. Making a change might be overwhelming or uncomfortable at first but so is growth. You may have to put in more money, effort, and time to reach your goal.

Bear in mind, one must be willing to change their behaviors to experience a different outcome. It is a great relief to know that you can make your life what you want it to be. If you need just one thing to do differently today than you did yesterday, make it this: Commit to taking 100% responsibility for every aspect of your life. Decide to make forward changes, one step at a time to envision your success.

> *"Change will not come if we wait for some other person or some other time. We are the ones we've been waiting for. We are the change that we seek."*
>
> *Barack Obama*

Barack Obama is a perfect example of a person who envisioned success when all odds were against him. When Obama was elected president, he inherited a failing economy, an ongoing war, and scrutiny beyond reproach. Some individuals cannot deal with changes or the stumbling blocks due to mental blocks of doubts. Some people also become overwhelmed or afraid of being successful and the thought of actually achieving their goals and desires.

> *"Our deepest fear is not that we are inadequate. Our deepest fear is that we are powerful beyond measure. It is our light, not our darkness, that most frightens us."*
>
> **Marianne Deborah Williamson**
> ─────────────────────────

What if you could become that famous actor or actress? What if you could become that district sales leader for a huge company? You have the power to become whomever you may want to be because vision is power. Every one of us has received some type of moral support or guidance from a positive person or family member. However, there are also dream killers who can sabotage your vision. You must protect your dreams and be willing to make daily affirmations to be successful.

Are some of your dreams of visions so astronomical that you cannot share them? If your dreams don't scare you, they are not big enough. Some of the things that you want to accomplish should not be shared with others. Only the universe and a higher power should know all the things that you want to accomplish.

Okay let's face it, all dreams and visions do not come to fruition. However, you must also identify the stumbling blocks that may be in front of you. Turn your deepest wish into a goal and turn that goal into a power statement. Look back at your dream list and identify what is most important. Identify the obstacle that you must overcome and follow the most important steps to overcome them and achieve your goal.

Here is a list of subjects that will remind you of how to activate your vision.

❏ Don't forget to write your vision down
❏ Write down your negative thoughts about your vision and crush them
❏ Be clear and understand your stumbling blocks
❏ Declare action dates

SHELTON FOREMAN

CHAPTER SIX

AFFIRM YOURSELF

What if you awakened every morning with a positive mindset simply ready for whatever life would throw at you? Envisioning yourself successful and keeping a firm desire to succeed is all about mindset and affirmations. You should take the time to understand and to receive clarity of what you want and more importantly, why you want it.

A young man wanted to be an actor when he was growing up. Of course, he performed for his family and friends. However, he was shy and never felt like he measured up to others when it came down to being comedic or outgoing. He wrote scripts and jokes to tell all his friends. However, he did not begin to own his craft until he completely let go. He let go of his fear, allowing his faith and creativity to take over completely. He was no longer afraid of what people thought of his performance or his worth. He was only concerned with respecting with craft and his self-worth.

Maybe you're like this young man. Maybe you are afraid to affirm your dreams out of fear they will never happen. There is an infamous affirmation that states, "I AM". This affirmation could clearly change a life from negative to positive. You must choose affirmation statements that will resonate a specific goal or aim. Envision yourself already living your dream with vivid details and all the emotions that you may experience. Focus on staying positive while being mindful of living in the moment so you can enjoy the journey.

You have the desire to create all the success and

prosperity you may ever ask for. Affirmations are a part of proven success strategies that many haven't tapped into.

Life comes with turns and twist and may offer a series of unfortunate events. What do you do with the lessons and unfortunate events? Life's lessons can leave you bruised and bothered. Many people have an ideology that being strong is holding on. Letting go of the past and negative beliefs can promote a positive lifestyle and induce a positive outcome.

There is also power in negative thinking. What are you telling yourself every day? Sit down and think about your deepest desires. Now, say them aloud and create your own affirmation.

> *"Have a vision. It is the ability to see the invisible, you can achieve the impossible."*
>
> *Shiv Khera*

Each day has a newness, but forward thinking will help you achieve the impossible. Visionaries often affirm their thoughts through ritualistic practices, some of which have nothing to do with religion. Affirmations may include meditating, reading, or speaking positive thoughts.

Here is a list of affirmations that you can use to affirm yourself and your vision.

❏ My mind is open to exciting and new possibilities every day.

❏ I am worthy of all the good things that life has to offer

and I deserve to be successful.
- ❏ I believe in myself and my ability to succeed.
- ❏ I am grateful for all my talents and skills.
- ❏ The universe is filled with endless opportunities for me and my successful career.
- ❏ I am surrounded by positive, supportive people who believe in me.
- ❏ I am thankful that my earnings are doubling.

CHAPTER SEVEN

BE CONSTRUCTIVE

Some people have a belief that the power of the mind is enough to accomplish goals. I beg to differ. Every action requires another action to move forward. Believing in the possibilities of greatness is being constructive.

> *"The longer and the more desperately I tried, the more I came to the conviction that only the discovery of a universal formal principle could lead us to assured results."*
>
> *Albert Einstein*

The desire to be the ultimate fighter is more than a mind frame. You must know how to help yourself to accomplish goals seen and unseen. Everyone is not born with a silver spoon and some are not born with a teaspoon of optimism. However, they learn to keep striving during the uphill climb.

One young lady had a similar story. She was put up for adoption at an incredibly young age and never knew her parents. Unfortunately, the young girl was tossed from family to family and sometimes abused in the process. She never learned how to love and did not know how to be loved as a kid nor an adult. She did not understand the cards she was dealt, and no one would really listen. But she chose to be constructive, studying extremely hard in her scholastic studies, and music afforded her many opportunities. She kept her head high even when her doubts were high. She found her voice through music and allowed her pain to help rid her self-doubt. She later became a self-made millionaire with a family to share her love and care with.

What if she just quit or stopped being constructive. She listened to her inner voice and instincts when she became discouraged. Being constructive is not being self-destroying. As mentioned before, some people get used to telling themselves stories or accepting stories from others. Who told you that you are not good enough? Who told you that you cannot compete with others? Being constructive is simply being consistent, regardless of the stumbling blocks.

As kids, many of us had natural instincts not to give up. We played our favorite board games or game systems until we conquered a certain level so we could claim the winner's title. We were well aware of the stumbling blocks and what specific blocks we would face, but we did not let it stop us from trying. We can learn a lot from children and our humble childhood beginnings. We constructively handled problems and created solutions to solve problems accordingly. Ok, childhood problems were not as complicated, but the fear of not conquering them were not overwhelming.

There was once a fearless immigrant who came to the states to create a better life for herself and her family. She faced numerous stumbling blocks but kept trying because that's how badly she wanted success. She applied for several companies, but her desire was to work for the airlines. Seeing the world and working at the same time would be a dream come true for her. However, it took a year before she received a call back from any airline. She continued to dream of being that amazing flight attendant. One day, she received a call to interview with an industry-leading airline. Her passion showed through and she was offered a job immediately. Her provision and constructive dream became true because she never stopped trying. She was excited and more than elated that she received such an amazing offer.

Her small dream to see the world and to take care of her family all stated as a thought. Then she put the work in, applying, interviewing, and then passing the training. She conquered all stumbling blocks almost effortlessly.

After graduating, she was sent to work her first flight as second in command as a flight attendant. The young flight attendant was so excited, but she had no idea what she would face on her first day. The nervous flight attendant began her flight procedures when she noticed a guy with a gun about to hijack the plane at the emergency exit door. She grabbed the gun and pulled the hijacker out of the emergency exit. Without hesitation, she saved more than two hundred lives and prevented a plan from being hijacked by the terrorist. She was fearless and constructive.

Fighters are constructive and often don't have options to give up or to fall victim to issues. This flight attendant showed her commitment to her dream and the passengers. Not only did she not quit after her horrible experience, she still works for the company and does so resiliently.

What would you do if your beautiful dream turned into an unfortunate and nasty nightmare? Would you give up on your dream and stop being constructive in the planning process if your dream were deferred? There is so much power in knowing yourself and the power within. An individual being constructive can shape their destiny.

> *Your happiness depends on your everyday thoughts.*
>
> *Shelton Foreman*

Have you ever seen one of those mind teaser illusions? They will tease the brain into believing almost anything. One mindbender illustrated a train going in one direction at an extremely fast pace. However, the brain teaser asked the perceiver and/or viewer to think hard about the train going in the opposite direction. The perceiver immediately saw the train going the other way. A simple constructive thought can change an entire situation. We are all mentally powerful. If you think about a train moving in an opposite direction, you can imagine yourself writing a book, opening a new business, or buying that dream home. The only limits that exist surround your innermost thoughts.

Here is a list of subjects of major areas that can remind you to be constructive.

❑ Stay focused and live in this very moment.

❑ Resist the urge to rush the process of success.

❑ Stop doing purposeless things that do not make yourself happy.

❑ Let go of guilt and enjoy every second that you live.

CHAPTER EIGHT

ACCEPTING THE WIN

Today, what do you feel like you deserve from all your efforts or goal planning? We have all experienced our share of winning moments and defeating moments in life. Maybe being turned down for a dream job or losing hope after failing a test you studied hard for.

> *"When things go wrong, as they sometimes will,*
> *When the road you're trudging seems all uphill,*
> *When the funds are low and the debts are high,*
> *And you want to smile, but you have to sigh,*
> *When care is pressing you down a bit,*
> *Rest if you must, but don't you quit."*
> **Author Unknown**

We have all heard about winning and losing gracefully. Accepting the upward approach to any situation can invite a person to the winners' circle. It is all about emotions and controlling those emotions, whether you're winning or losing. Some people are taught that winning is a part of every sector of their lives. It is especially important to keep your perspective when seeking to accomplish certain goals.

True fighters sometimes do not think about losing, but they are aware of their opponent. However, being a fighter does not mean losing yourself while training to win.

A perfect example would be Jarvis, who grew up in a foster home where he was constantly abused both verbally and physically. He excelled in the classroom but, he never enjoyed his childhood or learned how to interact with other children. After high school, he was accepted into a reputable college and was granted an opportunity to live on campus. Learning how to put things in their proper place and enjoying life were incredibly challenging for him. However, he grasped the idea of how to successfully communicate with others by being elected as a vice president on the student council.

Simply opening himself up to win and being optimistic helped him win many opportunities in his adulthood. He had a hard time understanding why his past was hard but made sure that the things he could control in his adult life were grand. He accepted the things he could not change and built upon his weaknesses.

Many individuals cannot win because they cannot let go of prior hurts and strife. Some life fighters have a hard time understanding that letting go is winning at times. It doesn't matter your religion, creed, or sex, you must understand that life is not going to always place you in winning positions. Learning how to accept the downs, ups, and the heartaches will lead you to a life of clarity. Have the inertia and the belief in yourself that will allow you to go all the way.

Accepting the win is a part of self-acceptance. Accept your flaws, strengths, and power. May the power within you be released to do great things. There is a certain power that we all possess to do amazing things. I hope this book has equipped you to exert the power of the fighter within you. You deserve it.

> *"You're not a weak person and yes you're brave and bold. Strong people get up and face our worst fears every day and we keep on fighting."*
>
> **Shelton Foreman**

THE POWER OF THE FIGHTER

SHELTON FOREMAN

ABOUT THE AUTHOR

Shelton Foreman is a seasoned realtor and the Founder of Dream Elite Properties, a real estate brokerage firm that deals with residential and commercial real estate in Atlanta. He connects people to their dream homes with no fuss or headaches. His innovative solutions have helped countless clients achieve their real estate aspirations.

Well known for his unwavering devotion to meeting his clients' needs and his extensive market knowledge, Shelton attributes his 15-year career success mostly to positive referrals and repeat clients.

Shelton is the realtor of choice for any individual, developer or investor interested in Atlanta's most coveted properties. He combines great work ethic, unquestionable integrity, and exemplary service to offer the greatest possible value to his clients.

Having earned a business degree and an MBA, Shelton understands the technical part of dealing properties. He always ready to offer his clients solid advice and educate them on current market trends and data.

Shelton devotes his free time and efforts to philanthropy. He has helped many people, charities, and local organizations. He also enjoys acting, sports, and spending quality time with friends and family.

Shelton understands that selling or buying a house is important to you, thus he makes it his absolute priority!

THE POWER OF THE FIGHTER

SHELTON FOREMAN

www.ingramcontent.com/pod-product-compliance
Lightning Source LLC
Chambersburg PA
CBHW071316110426
42743CB00042B/2685